# MON CAHIER D'ÉCRITURE

## J'APPRENDS À LIRE ET À ÉCRIRE MONTESSORI

# My Sight Word List

French - Greek

| | | |
|---|---|---|
| a | in | said |
| and | is | see |
| away | it | the |
| big | jump | three |
| blue | little | to |
| can | look | two |
| come | make | up |
| down | me | we |
| find | my | where |
| for | not | yellow |
| funny | one | you |
| go | day | |
| help | play | |
| here | red | |
| I | run | |

Name: ____________________ Date: ____________________

Today is: Monday | Tuesday | Wednesday | Thursday | Friday

Direction: Trace and read the sentences.

| amusement | pistolet | courir | soleil |
| --- | --- | --- | --- |
|  | 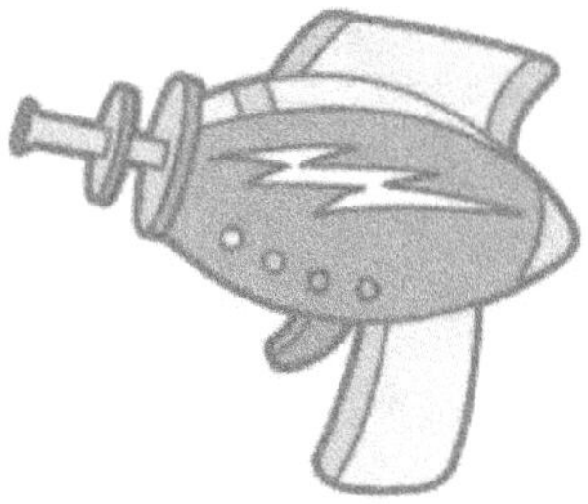 |  |  |
| διασκέδαση | όπλο | τρέξιμο | ήλιος |

They are having fun.

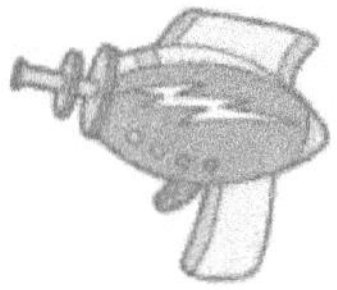

He has a gun.

The bear is running.

The sun is smiling.

Draw a Picture

I Can...

☐ use a Capital Letter
The cat is big.

☐ use spaces

☐ sound out words
d-o-g = dog

☐ use a Period .

☐ Draw a picture

He is having fun, running under the sun with his new toy gun.

| amusement | pistolet | courir | soleil |
|---|---|---|---|
| διασκέδαση | όπλο | τρέξιμο | ήλιος |

Name: _________________ Date: _______

Today is: Monday | Tuesday | Wednesday
Thursday | Friday

Direction: Trace and read the sentences.

| sac | chiffon | étiquette | remuer |
|---|---|---|---|
| τσάντα | κουρέλι | ετικέτα | κουνώντας |

He has many bags.

I see a rag.

I see a tag.

Its tail is wagging.

Draw a Picture

## I Can...

- [ ] use a Capital Letter
  The cat is big.
- [ ] use spaces
- [ ] sound out words
  d-o-g = dog
- [ ] use a Period .
- [ ] Draw a picture

The bag on the rag has a blue tag which made the dog's tail wag.

| sac | chiffon | étiquette | remuer |
|---|---|---|---|
| τσάντα | κουρέλι | ετικέτα | κουνώντας |

Name: _______________ Date: _______

Today is: [Monday] [Tuesday] [Wednesday]
[Thursday] [Friday]

Direction: Trace and read the sentences.

| canettes | homme | la poêle | van |
|---|---|---|---|
| κουτιά | άνδρας | τηγάνι | βαν |

I see a can of soda.

The man is happy.

The pan is dirty.

I see a big van.

Draw a Picture

## I Can...

- [ ] use a Capital Letter
  <u>T</u>he cat is big.

- [ ] use spaces

- [ ] sound out words
  d-o-g = dog

- [ ] use a Period .

- [ ] Draw a picture

The man who was driving a van ran over a can and a pan.

| canettes | homme | la poêle | van |
|---|---|---|---|
| κουτιά | άνδρας | τηγάνι | βαν |

Name: _________________________ Date: _______________

Today is: Monday | Tuesday | Wednesday
Thursday | Friday

Direction: Trace and read the sentences.

| couper | intestin | cabane | écrou |
|---|---|---|---|
| τομή | έντερο | καλύβα | καρύδι |

He cut his nails.

He has a gut.

This is a small hut.

It is holding a nut.

<table>
<tr><td>

**Draw a Picture**

</td><td>

## I Can...

☐ use a Capital Letter
<u>T</u>he cat is big.

☐ use spaces

☐ sound out words
  d-o-g = dog

☐ use a Period .

☐ Draw a picture

</td></tr>
</table>

A boy swallowed a nut and
it got stuck in his belly.
He had to get his gut
cut open in the hut.

| couper | intestin | cabane | écrou |
|---|---|---|---|
| τομή | έντερο | καλύβα | καρύδι |

Name: _______________ Date: _______________

Today is:  Monday   Tuesday   Wednesday
           Thursday   Friday

Direction: Trace and read the sentences.

| graisse | chat | chapeau | tapis |
|---|---|---|---|
| λίπος | γάτα | καπέλο | χαλάκι |

I see a fat dog.

This is my little cat.

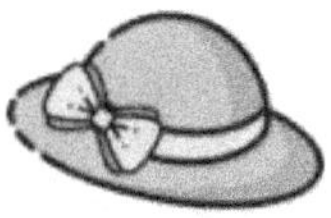

I like this hat.

I see a big mat.

Draw a Picture

I Can...

☐ use a Capital Letter
The cat is big.

☐ use spaces

☐ sound out words
d-o-g = dog

☐ use a Period .

☐ Draw a
picture

The fat cat laid on the
mat that was a hat
pattern.

| graisse | chat | chapeau | tapis |
|---|---|---|---|
| λίπος | γάτα | καπέλο | χαλάκι |

Name: ____________________ Date: ____________________

Today is: Monday Tuesday Wednesday Thursday Friday

Direction: Trace and read the sentences.

| taxi | laboratoire | languette | crabe |
| --- | --- | --- | --- |
|   |  | 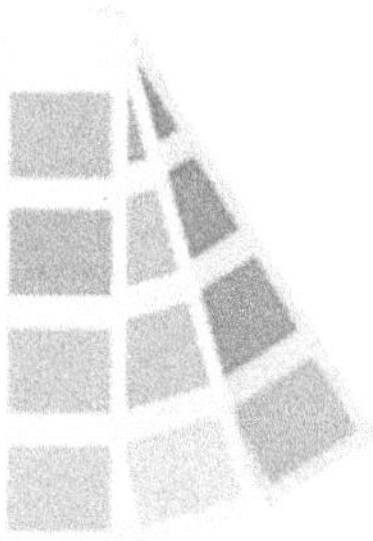 |  |
| ταξί | εργαστήριο | αυτί | κάβουρας |

The cab is fast.

The lab is exciting.

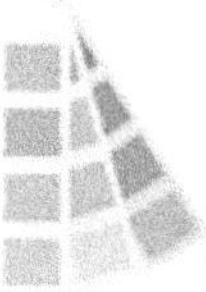

The tab is long.

We found a crab.

Name



## I Can...

- [ ] use a Capital Letter
  <u>T</u>he cat is big.

- [ ] use spaces

- [ ] sound out words
  d-o-g = dog

- [ ] use a Period .

- [ ] Draw a picture

The crab called a cab to
drive him to the lab and
when he got off he paid
his tab.

| taxi | laboratoire | languette | crabe |
|---|---|---|---|
| ταξί | εργαστήριο | αυτί | κάβουρας |

Name: ______________________ Date: ______________________

Today is: Monday Tuesday Wednesday Thursday Friday

Direction: Trace and read the sentences.

| jambon | confiture | mouton | palourde |
|---|---|---|---|
|  |  |  |  |
| ζαμπόν | μαρμελάδα | πρόβατο | αχιβάδα |

 I like to eat ham.

 We like to eat jam.

 The ram is big.

 The clam is pretty.

Draw a Picture

## I Can...

- [ ] use a Capital Letter
  The cat is big.

- [ ] use spaces

- [ ] sound out words
  d-o-g = dog

- [ ] use a Period .

- [ ] Draw a picture

The clam gave the ram ham. Then the ram gave the clam jam.

| jambon | confiture | mouton | palourde |
|---|---|---|---|
| ζαμπόν | μαρμελάδα | πρόβατο | αχιβάδα |

Name: ____________________ Date: ____________________

Today is: Monday Tuesday Wednesday Thursday Friday

Direction: Trace and read the sentences.

| lit | de premier plan | rouge | mariage |
|---|---|---|---|
| 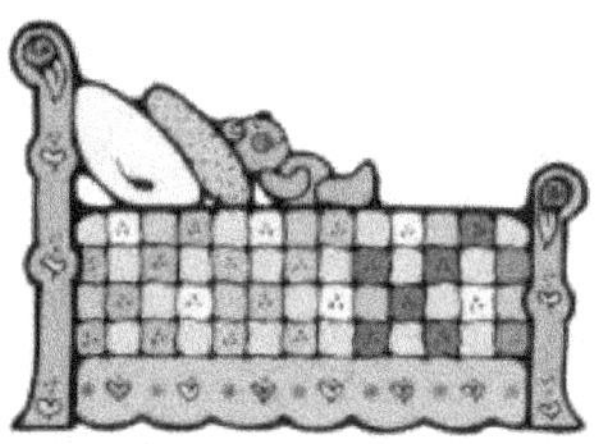 | 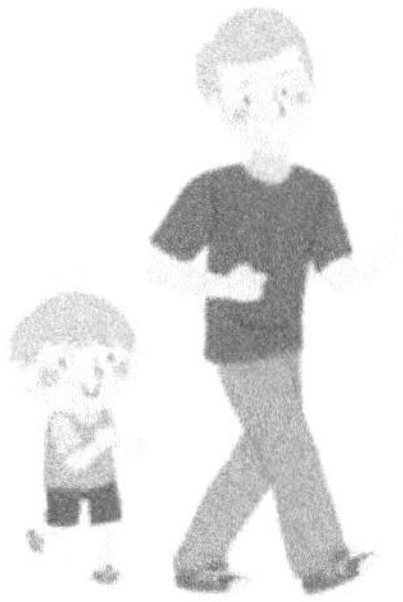 | 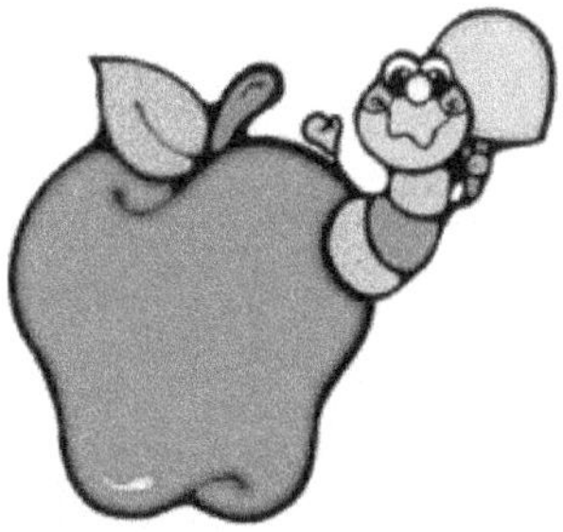 | 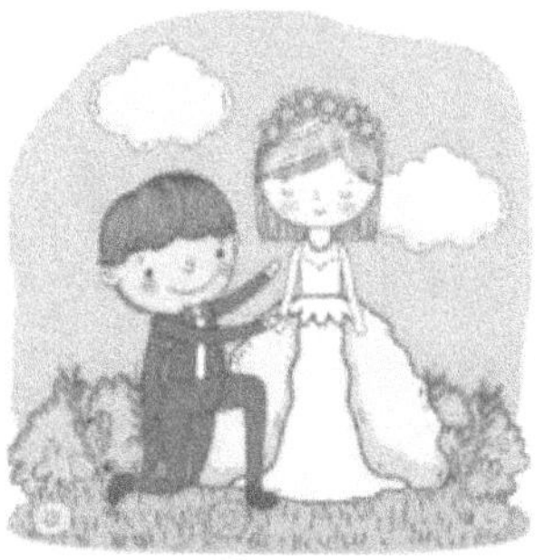 |
| κρεβάτι | κύριος | το κόκκινο | γάμος |

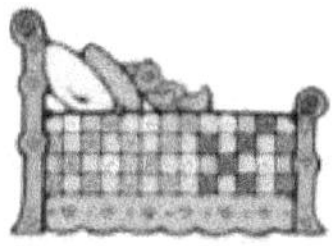

This is my little bed.

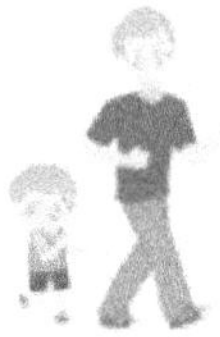

He led us to safety.

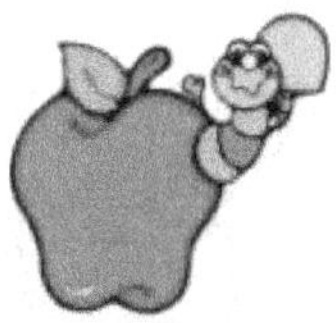

The apple is red.

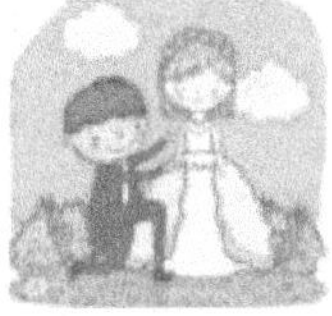

He asks her to wed.

## Draw a Picture

## I Can...

- [ ] use a Capital Letter
  <u>T</u>he cat is big.
- [ ] use spaces
- [ ] sound out words
  d-o-g = dog
- [ ] use a Period .
- [ ] Draw a picture

When the prince got out of bed, he was led on a red carpet to be wed with the princess.

| lit | de premier plan | rouge | mariage |
|---|---|---|---|
| κρεβάτι | κύριος | το κόκκινο | γάμος |

Name: ____________________ Date: ____________________

Today is: Monday Tuesday Wednesday Thursday Friday

Direction: Trace and read the sentences.

| mauvais | papa | furieux | triste |
| --- | --- | --- | --- |
|  |  |  |  |
| κακό | μπαμπάς | τρελός | λυπημένος |

 This apple is bad.

 My dad is very kind.

 The reindeer is mad.

 The little cat is sad.

I was bad so my dad
got mad and now
I am so sad.

| mauvais | papa | furieux | triste |
|---|---|---|---|
| κακό | μπαμπάς | τρελός | λυπημένος |

Name: _______________ Date: _______________

Today is: Monday  Tuesday  Wednesday  Thursday  Friday

Direction: Trace and read the sentences.

| animal den | poule | écuries | dix |
|---|---|---|---|
| φωλιά | κότα | στάβλοι | δέκα |

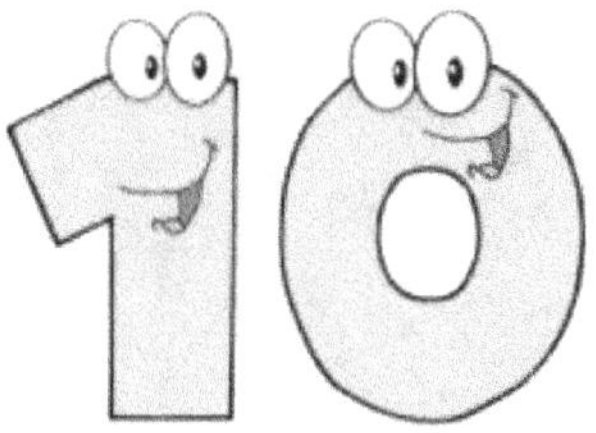

It is a den.

The hens lay eggs.

She has a good pen.

The ten is smiling.

Draw a Picture

I Can...

use a Capital Letter
The cat is big.

use spaces

sound out words
d-o-g = dog

use a Period .

Draw a
picture

The hen that lived in the
pen laid ten eggs
in her den.

| animal den | poule | écuries | dix |
|---|---|---|---|
| φωλιά | κότα | στάβλοι | δέκα |

Name: ____________________ Date: ____________________

Today is: Monday Tuesday Wednesday Thursday Friday

Direction: Trace and read the sentences.

| gommeux | maman | somme | tambour |
|---|---|---|---|
|  |  |   |  |
| κολλώδης | μαμά | άθροισμα | τύμπανο |

I like to chew gum.

My mum is kind!

I can do a sum!

The drum is big.

Mum was chewing gum while figuring out the sum of the drum's price.

| gommeux | maman | somme | tambour |
|---|---|---|---|
| κολλώδης | μαμά | άθροισμα | τύμπανο |

Name: _________________ Date: _____________

Today is: Monday | Tuesday | Wednesday
Thursday | Friday

Direction: Trace and read the sentences.

| offre | cacher | enfant | couvercle |
| --- | --- | --- | --- |
| προσφορά | κρύβω | παιδί | καπάκι |

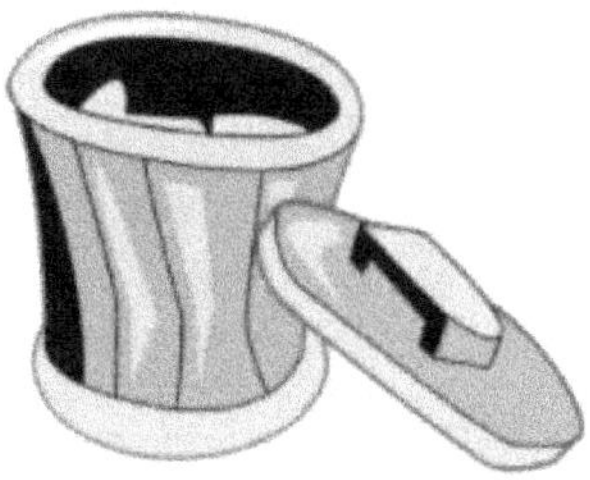

He likes to bid.

He is hiding.

The kid like to play.

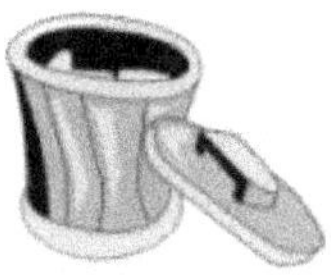

I see a lid.

Draw a Picture

## I Can...

- [ ] use a Capital Letter
  The cat is big.

- [ ] use spaces

- [ ] sound out words
  d-o-g = dog

- [ ] use a Period .

- [ ] Draw a picture

The kid bid a lid for one hundred dollars then hid from his mad parents.

| offre | cacher | enfant | couvercle |
|---|---|---|---|
| προσφορά | κρύβω | παιδί | καπάκι |

Name: ____________________ Date: ____________________

Today is: Monday Tuesday Wednesday Thursday Friday

Direction: Trace and read the sentences.

| gros | creuser | porc | perruque |
| --- | --- | --- | --- |
|  |  |  |  |
| μεγάλο | σκάβω | χοίρος | περούκα |

That is a big pencil.

He will dig up a hole.

The pig is fat.

She puts on a wig.

Name _______________________

## Draw a Picture

## I Can...

☐ use a Capital Letter
The cat is big.

☐ use spaces

☐ sound out words
d-o-g = dog

☐ use a Period .

☐ Draw a picture

The big pig went to dig in the mud for his wig.

| gros | creuser | porc | perruque |
|---|---|---|---|
| μεγάλο | σκάβω | χοίρος | περούκα |

Name: _________________________ Date: _____________

Today is:  Monday   Tuesday   Wednesday

Thursday   Friday

Direction: Trace and read the sentences.

| poubelle | ailette | épingle | gagner |
|---|---|---|---|
| αποθήκη | πτερύγιο | καρφίτσα | νίκη |

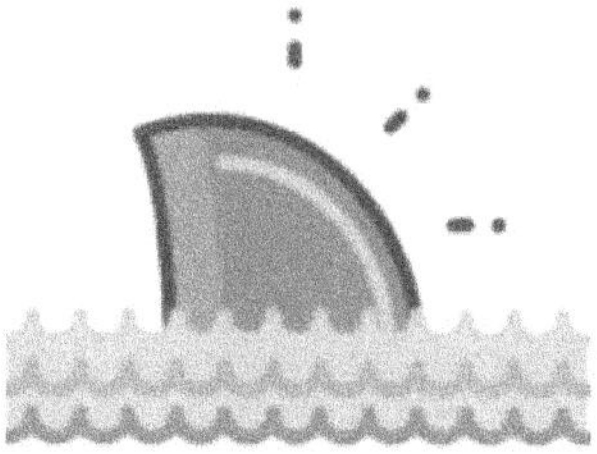

It is a recycle bin.

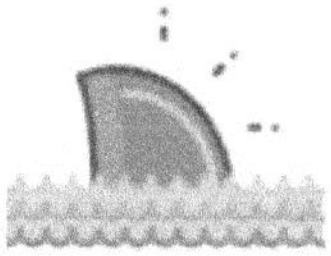

The shark has a fin.

The pin is pointy.

He won the match.

Draw a Picture

## I Can...

- [ ] use a Capital Letter
  <u>T</u>he cat is big.

- [ ] use spaces

- [ ] sound out words
  d-o-g = dog

- [ ] use a Period .

- [ ] Draw a picture

The dangerous fin of the fish was pinned to the bin. Then the sailors had a contest on who will win by touching the fin the longest.

Name: _______________ Date: _______

Today is:  [ Monday ] [ Tuesday ] [ Wednesday ]
[ Thursday ] [ Friday ]

Direction: Trace and read the sentences.

| hanche | lèvres | pincer | boisson |
|---|---|---|---|

| ισχίο | χείλια | τσιμπώ | ποτό |
|---|---|---|---|

This is my hip.

Her lips are red.

It is nipping its toy.

She is sipping.

Name

Draw a Picture

## I Can...

- [ ] use a Capital Letter
  <u>T</u>he cat is big.

- [ ] use spaces

- [ ] sound out words
  d-o-g = dog

- [ ] use a Period .

- [ ] Draw a
  picture

The dog nipped someone
who was sipping water
with his lip.

| hanche | lèvres | pincer | boisson |
|--------|--------|--------|---------|
| ισχίο | χείλια | τσιμπώ | ποτό |

Name: _________________  Date: _____________

Today is: 

Direction: Trace and read the sentences.

| **en forme** | **frappé** | **trousse** | **asseoir** |
|---|---|---|---|
| κατάλληλος | κτύπημα | σύνεργα | καθίστε |

It is perfectly fit.

They hit each other.

That is a safety kit.

He is sitting.

Name

## Draw a Picture

## I Can...

- [ ] use a Capital Letter
  <u>T</u>he cat is big.

- [ ] use spaces

- [ ] sound out words
  d-o-g = dog

- [ ] use a Period .

- [ ] Draw a picture

The fit doctor sat then was hit by a kit.

| **en forme** | **frappé** | **trousse** | **asseoir** |
|---|---|---|---|
| κατάλληλος | κτύπημα | σύνεργα | καθίστε |

Name: ______________________ Date: ______________________

Today is: Monday Tuesday Wednesday Thursday Friday

Direction: Trace and read the sentences.

| blé | emploi | rob | pleurer |
| --- | --- | --- | --- |
|  |  |  |  |
| καλαμπόκι | δουλειά | ληστεύω | κραυγή |

 I ate corn on the cob.

 This is my job.

 He is robbing.

 The girl is sobbing.

Draw a Picture

## I Can...

- [ ] use a Capital Letter
  <u>T</u>he cat is big.
- [ ] use spaces
- [ ] sound out words
  d-o-g = dog
- [ ] use a Period .
- [ ] Draw a picture

The chef robbed a corn cob and then was sobbing because he had lost his job.

| blé | emploi | rob | pleurer |
|---|---|---|---|
| καλαμπόκι | δουλειά | ληστεύω | κραυγή |

Name: ____________________ Date: ____________________

Today is: Monday | Tuesday | Wednesday | Thursday | Friday

Direction: Trace and read the sentences.

| chien | porc | le jogging | bois |
| --- | --- | --- | --- |
|  |  |  | 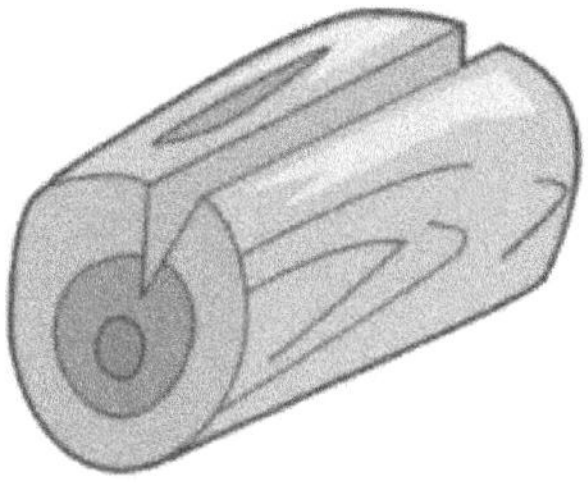 |
| σκύλος | γουρούνι | τζόκινγκ | ξύλο |

The dog is thrilled.

The hog is big.

She is jogging.

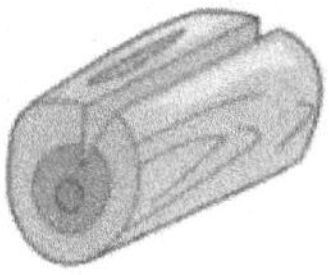

The log is small.

Draw a Picture

## I Can...

- [ ] use a Capital Letter
  The cat is big.
- [ ] use spaces
- [ ] sound out words
  d-o-g = dog
- [ ] use a Period .
- [ ] Draw a picture

The dog and the hog went for a jog but then tripped on a log.

| chien | porc | le jogging | bois |
|---|---|---|---|
| σκύλος | γουρούνι | τζόκινγκ | ξύλο |

Name: _______________ Date: _______

Today is: Monday   Tuesday   Wednesday

Thursday   Friday

Direction: Trace and read the sentences.

| punaise | étreinte | cruche | agresser |
|---|---|---|---|
| έντομο | αγκαλιάζω | κανάτα | κούπα |

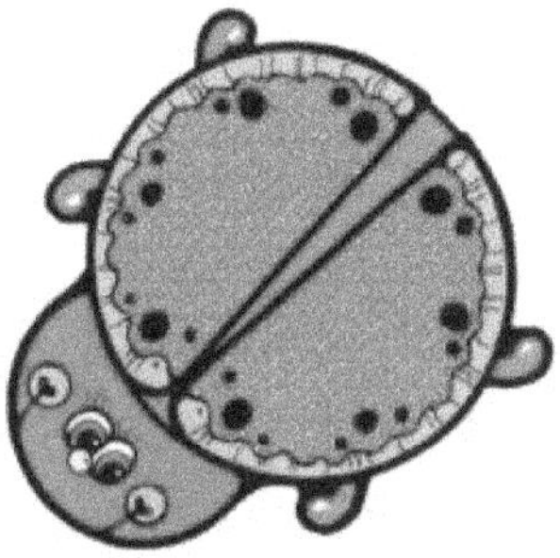

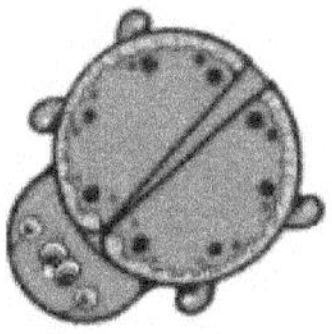

The bug is colorful.

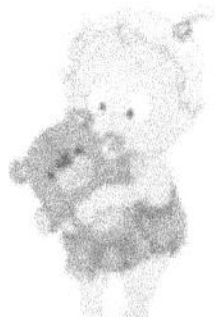

She is hugging.

The jug has milk in it.

He has a mug.

Draw a Picture

## I Can...

- [ ] use a Capital Letter
  The cat is big.
- [ ] use spaces
- [ ] sound out words
  d-o-g = dog
- [ ] use a Period .
- [ ] Draw a picture

The bug hugged the jug and the mug which was full of jam.

| punaise | étreinte | cruche | agresser |
| --- | --- | --- | --- |
| έντομο | αγκαλιάζω | κανάτα | κούπα |

Name: ____________________ Date: ____________________

Today is: Monday Tuesday Wednesday Thursday Friday

Direction: Trace and read the sentences.

| lit | point | chaud | pot |
|---|---|---|---|
| 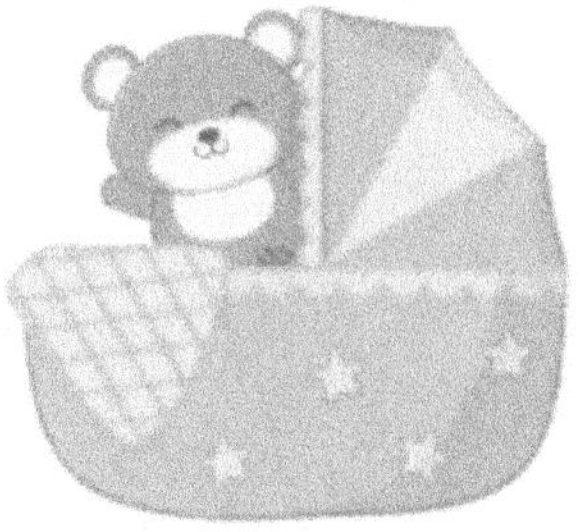 | 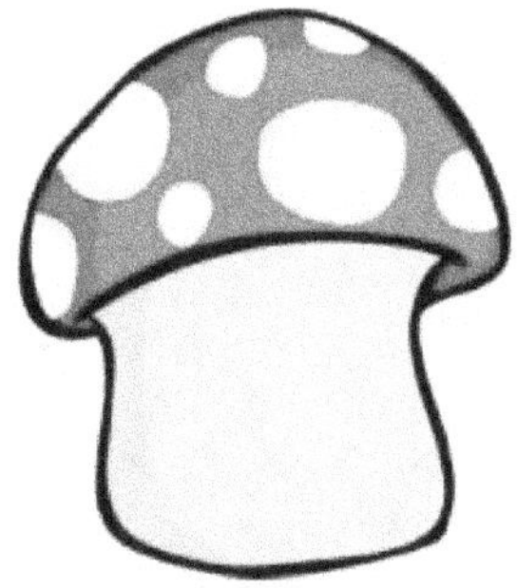 | 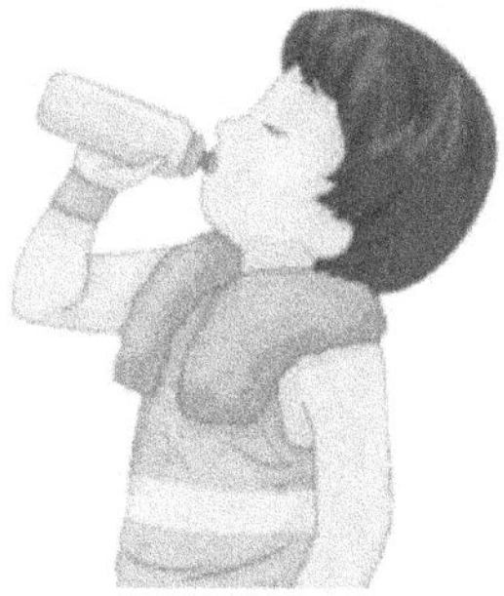 | 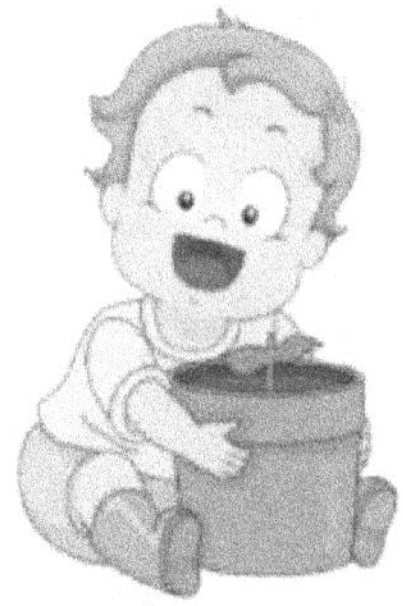 |
| κρεβάτι | τελεία | ζεστό | δοχείο |

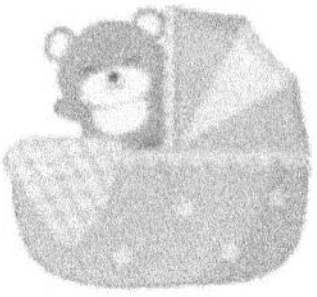

This is my cot.

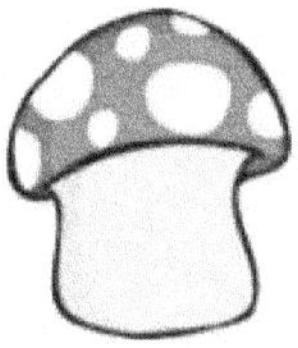

There are many dots.

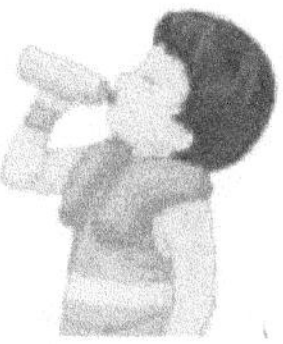

It is very hot.

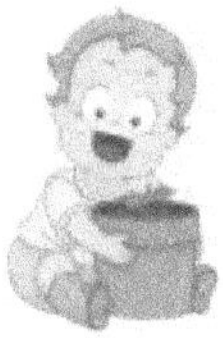

He has a plant pot.

Name

Draw a Picture

## I Can...

- [ ] use a Capital Letter
  <u>T</u>he cat is big.

- [ ] use spaces

- [ ] sound out words
  d-o-g = dog

- [ ] use a Period .

- [ ] Draw a picture

The baby climbed out of the cot with the dot pattern and ate the hot pot.

| lit | point | chaud | pot |
|-----|-------|-------|-----|
| κρεβάτι | τελεία | ζεστό | δοχείο |

Name: _________________________  Date: _______________

Today is: [ Monday ] [ Tuesday ] [ Wednesday ]
[ Thursday ] [ Friday ]

Direction: Read the words and make a sentence.

| amusement | pistolet | courir | soleil |
|---|---|---|---|
| διασκέδαση | όπλο | τρέξιμο | ήλιος |

Name

Draw a Picture

## I Can...

- [ ] use a Capital Letter
The cat is big.

- [ ] use spaces

- [ ] sound out words
d-o-g = dog

- [ ] use a Period .

- [ ] Draw a picture

Name: _______________________ Date: _______________

Today is: Monday  Tuesday  Wednesday

Thursday  Friday

Name: _______________________  Date: _______________

Today is: [Monday] [Tuesday] [Wednesday] [Thursday] [Friday]

Direction: Read the words and make a sentence.

| sac | chiffon | étiquette | remuer |
|-----|---------|-----------|--------|
| τσάντα | κουρέλι | ετικέτα | κουνώντας |

Name ___________________________

Draw a Picture

## I Can...

- [ ] use a Capital Letter
  The cat is big.

- [ ] use spaces

- [ ] sound out words
  d-o-g = dog

- [ ] use a Period .

- [ ] Draw a picture

Name: _______________________ Date: _______________

Today is: [ Monday ] [ Tuesday ] [ Wednesday ] [ Thursday ] [ Friday ]

Name: _______________________  Date: _______________________

Today is:  Monday   Tuesday   Wednesday

Thursday   Friday

Direction: Read the words and make a sentence.

| canettes | homme | la poêle | van |
| --- | --- | --- | --- |
| κουτιά | άνδρας | τηγάνι | βαν |

Name

Draw a Picture

## I Can...

☐ use a Capital Letter
The cat is big.

☐ use spaces

☐ sound out words
d-o-g = dog

☐ use a Period .

☐ Draw a picture

Name: _______________________  Date: _______________

Today is: | Monday | Tuesday | Wednesday |
| Thursday | Friday |

Today is: Monday | Tuesday | Wednesday | Thursday | Friday

Direction: Read the words and make a sentence.

| couper | intestin | cabane | écrou |
|---|---|---|---|
| τομή | έντερο | καλύβα | καρύδι |

Name

Draw a Picture

## I Can...

☐ use a Capital Letter
The cat is big.

☐ use spaces

☐ sound out words
d-o-g = dog

☐ use a Period .

☐ Draw a picture

Name: _______________________ Date: _______________________

Today is: Monday  Tuesday  Wednesday  Thursday  Friday

Name: _________________________  Date: _______________

Today is:  Monday   Tuesday   Wednesday

Thursday   Friday

Direction: Read the words and make a sentence.

| graisse | chat | chapeau | tapis |
|---|---|---|---|
| λίπος | γάτα | καπέλο | χαλάκι |

# Name

Draw a Picture

## I Can...

- [ ] use a Capital Letter
  <u>T</u>he cat is big.

- [ ] use spaces

- [ ] sound out words
  d-o-g = dog

- [ ] use a Period .

- [ ] Draw a picture

Name: _______________________    Date: _____________

Today is: | Monday | Tuesday | Wednesday |
| Thursday | Friday |

Name: _____________________  Date: _____________________

Today is: Monday  Tuesday  Wednesday  Thursday  Friday

Direction: Read the words and make a sentence.

| taxi | laboratoire | languette | crabe |
|------|-------------|-----------|-------|
| ταξί | εργαστήριο | αυτί | κάβουρας |

Name

Draw a Picture

## I Can...

- [ ] use a Capital Letter
  The cat is big.

- [ ] use spaces

- [ ] sound out words
  d-o-g = dog

- [ ] use a Period  .

- [ ] Draw a picture

Name: _________________  Date: _________________

Today is: Monday | Tuesday | Wednesday

Thursday | Friday

Name: ______________________ Date: ______________

Today is: Monday  Tuesday  Wednesday

Thursday  Friday

Direction: Read the words and make a sentence.

| jambon | confiture | mouton | palourde |
|---|---|---|---|
| ζαμπόν | μαρμελάδα | πρόβατο | αχιβάδα |

Name

## Draw a Picture

## I Can...

- [ ] use a Capital Letter
  The cat is big.

- [ ] use spaces

- [ ] sound out words
  d-o-g = dog

- [ ] use a Period .

- [ ] Draw a picture

Name: _________________    Date: _________

Today is: Monday | Tuesday | Wednesday
Thursday | Friday

Name: _______________________ Date: _______________

Today is: [ Monday ] [ Tuesday ] [ Wednesday ]
[ Thursday ] [ Friday ]

Direction: Read the words and make a sentence.

| lit | de premier plan | rouge | mariage |
| --- | --- | --- | --- |
| κρεβάτι | κύριος | το κόκκινο | γάμος |

Name

Draw a Picture

## I Can...

- [ ] use a Capital Letter
  <u>T</u>he cat is big.

- [ ] use spaces

- [ ] sound out words
  d-o-g = dog

- [ ] use a Period .

- [ ] Draw a picture

Name: _______________________ Date: _______________

Today is: Monday Tuesday Wednesday Thursday Friday

Name: _______________________  Date: _______________

Today is: [ Monday ] [ Tuesday ] [ Wednesday ]
[ Thursday ] [ Friday ]

Direction: Read the words and make a sentence.

| mauvais | papa | furieux | triste |
|---|---|---|---|
| κακό | μπαμπάς | τρελός | λυπημένος |

<u>Name</u>

Draw a Picture

## I Can...

- [ ] use a Capital Letter
  <u>T</u>he cat is big.

- [ ] use spaces

- [ ] sound out words
  d-o-g = dog

- [ ] use a Period .

- [ ] Draw a picture

Name: _______________________   Date: _______________

Today is: Monday  Tuesday  Wednesday  Thursday  Friday

Name: ____________________ Date: ____________________

Today is: Monday | Tuesday | Wednesday | Thursday | Friday

Direction: Read the words and make a sentence.

| | | | |
|---|---|---|---|
| **animal den** | **poule** | **écuries** | **dix** |
|  |  |  |  |
| φωλιά | κότα | στάβλοι | δέκα |

Name ______________________________

Draw a Picture

## I Can...

☐ use a Capital Letter
The cat is big.

☐ use spaces

☐ sound out words
d-o-g = dog

☐ use a Period .

☐ Draw a picture

Name: _________________ Date: _________________

Today is: Monday  Tuesday  Wednesday

Thursday  Friday

Name: _______________ Date: _______________

Today is: Monday  Tuesday  Wednesday  Thursday  Friday

Direction: Read the words and make a sentence.

| **gommeux** | **maman** | **somme** | **tambour** |
| κολλώδης | μαμά | άθροισμα | τύμπανο |

# Name

Draw a Picture

## I Can...

- [ ] use a Capital Letter
  The cat is big.
- [ ] use spaces
- [ ] sound out words
  d-o-g = dog
- [ ] use a Period .
- [ ] Draw a picture

Name: _______________________  Date: _______________________

Today is:  Monday   Tuesday   Wednesday   Thursday   Friday

Name: _________________________  Date: _______________

Today is: [ Monday ] [ Tuesday ] [ Wednesday ]
[ Thursday ] [ Friday ]

Direction: Read the words and make a sentence.

| offre | cacher | enfant | couvercle |
| --- | --- | --- | --- |
| προσφορά | κρύβω | παιδί | καπάκι |

Name

Draw a Picture

## I Can...

- [ ] use a Capital Letter
  The cat is big.

- [ ] use spaces

- [ ] sound out words
  d-o-g = dog

- [ ] use a Period .

- [ ] Draw a picture

Name: ___________________  Date: ___________

Today is: Monday  Tuesday  Wednesday  Thursday  Friday

Name: _______________________  Date: _______________

Today is: [Monday] [Tuesday] [Wednesday]
[Thursday] [Friday]

Direction: Read the words and make a sentence.

| **gros** | **creuser** | **porc** | **perruque** |
|---|---|---|---|
| μεγάλο | σκάβω | χοίρος | περούκα |

Name

Draw a Picture

## I Can...

☐ use a Capital Letter
The cat is big.

☐ use spaces

☐ sound out words
d-o-g = dog

☐ use a Period .

☐ Draw a picture

Name: _______________    Date: _______________

Today is: Monday  Tuesday  Wednesday
          Thursday  Friday

Name: ____________________ Date: ____________________

Today is: Monday Tuesday Wednesday Thursday Friday

Direction: Read the words and make a sentence.

| poubelle | ailette | épingle | gagner |
| --- | --- | --- | --- |
|   | 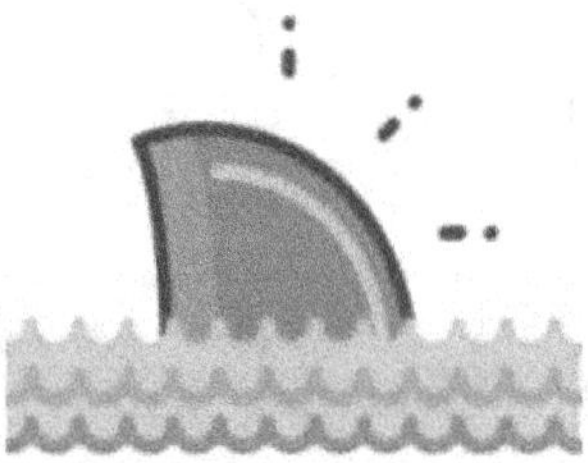 |  |  |
| αποθήκη | πτερύγιο | καρφίτσα | νίκη |

____________________

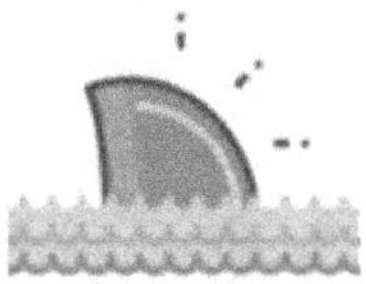

____________________

____________________

____________________

Name

Draw a Picture

## I Can...

- [ ] use a Capital Letter
  The cat is big.

- [ ] use spaces

- [ ] sound out words
  d-o-g = dog

- [ ] use a Period  .

- [ ] Draw a picture

Name:_____________________ Date:_____________

Today is: Monday Tuesday Wednesday Thursday Friday

Name: _________________________ Date: _______________

Today is: [ Monday ] [ Tuesday ] [ Wednesday ]
[ Thursday ] [ Friday ]

Direction: Read the words and make a sentence.

| hanche | lèvres | pincer | boisson |
|---|---|---|---|
| ισχίο | χείλια | τσιμπώ | ποτό |

Name ____________________

Draw a Picture

## I Can...

- [ ] use a Capital Letter
  The cat is big.

- [ ] use spaces

- [ ] sound out words
  d-o-g = dog

- [ ] use a Period .

- [ ] Draw a picture

Name: _____________________    Date: _____________

Today is: Monday  Tuesday  Wednesday  Thursday  Friday

Name: ___________________  Date: ___________________

Today is: [ Monday ] [ Tuesday ] [ Wednesday ]
[ Thursday ] [ Friday ]

Direction: Read the words and make a sentence.

| en forme | frappé | trousse | asseoir |
|---|---|---|---|
| κατάλληλος | κτύπημα | σύνεργα | καθίστε |

Name

Draw a Picture

## I Can...

- [ ] use a Capital Letter
  The cat is big.

- [ ] use spaces

- [ ] sound out words
  d-o-g = dog

- [ ] use a Period .

- [ ] Draw a picture

Name: _______________  Date: _______________

Today is: Monday  Tuesday  Wednesday  Thursday  Friday

Name: _________________________  Date: _____________

Today is: [ Monday ] [ Tuesday ] [ Wednesday ]
[ Thursday ] [ Friday ]

Direction: Read the words and make a sentence.

| blé | emploi | rob | pleurer |
|---|---|---|---|
| καλαμπόκι | δουλειά | ληστεύω | κραυγή |

Name

Draw a Picture

I Can...

☐ use a Capital Letter
The cat is big.

☐ use spaces

☐ sound out words
d-o-g = dog

☐ use a Period .

☐ Draw a
picture

Name: ___________________  Date: ___________________

Today is: Monday  Tuesday  Wednesday
Thursday  Friday

Name: ________________  Date: ________________

Today is: [Monday] [Tuesday] [Wednesday]
[Thursday] [Friday]

Direction: Read the words and make a sentence.

| chien | porc | le jogging | bois |
|---|---|---|---|
| σκύλος | γουρούνι | τζόκινγκ | ξύλο |

Name

Draw a Picture

## I Can...

- [ ] use a Capital Letter
  The cat is big.

- [ ] use spaces

- [ ] sound out words
  d-o-g = dog

- [ ] use a Period .

- [ ] Draw a picture

Name: ________________  Date: __________

Today is:  Monday  Tuesday  Wednesday  Thursday  Friday

| punaise | étreinte | cruche | agresser |
|---|---|---|---|
| έντομο | αγκαλιάζω | κανάτα | κούπα |

Name

Draw a Picture

## I Can...

- [ ] use a Capital Letter
  The cat is big.

- [ ] use spaces

- [ ] sound out words
  d-o-g = dog

- [ ] use a Period .

- [ ] Draw a picture

Name: _______________________  Date: _______________

Today is: Monday  Tuesday  Wednesday  Thursday  Friday

Name: _______________________  Date: _______________________

Today is: [Monday] [Tuesday] [Wednesday]
[Thursday] [Friday]

Direction: Read the words and make a sentence.

| lit | point | chaud | pot |
|---|---|---|---|
| κρεβάτι | τελεία | ζεστό | δοχείο |

Name

Draw a Picture

## I Can...

- [ ] use a Capital Letter
  The cat is big.

- [ ] use spaces

- [ ] sound out words
  d-o-g = dog

- [ ] use a Period .

- [ ] Draw a picture

Name: _____________________ Date: _____________________

Today is: Monday Tuesday Wednesday Thursday Friday